## The Romans

The city of Rome in central Italy was formed around 800 BCE and grew over the centuries into the Roman Empire, which covered large parts of Europe, the Middle East and North Africa. It was a highly sophisticated and technologically advanced society, with a large army, major roads and many cities. Britain at that time was a mysterious place with fierce tribes and valuable metals, which became the focus of an attempted invasion in 55 BCE and 54 BCE by *Julius Caesar*. Those invasions were only marginally successful and the Romans did not try again to invade Britain for almost 100 years. By 43 CE the *Emperor Claudius* decided to invade Britain, which was weakened by the death of *King Cunobelin* of the *Trinovantes*, who lived in *Camulodunum (Colchester)*. After attacking Colchester his forces then moved across England, including where present day Chichester is located...

*Visiting Chichester*
*Chichester lies about 82 miles (132 km) south-west of London. The Novium Museum has artefacts, mosaics and more, found in Chichester. Sections of the Roman Town Wall can be seen surrounding the city. A small information board showing the site of the Roman Amphitheatre can also be seen. For more information see page 32.*

4. Chichester 20 CE

*A speculative view of Chichester, looking north, 20 CE.*

# Chichester 20 CE

The Chichester area had long been occupied before the Roman invasion and had strong ties with continental Europe. Around 150 BCE *Belgic*[1] tribes occupied the lands of local British tribes in the south, having three main centres in Chichester, Winchester and Silchester *(a village near Basingstoke)*. These tribes became the *Atrebates* and kept trade links with the continent. In the years before the invasion, the tribes in the area which is now Essex and Hertfordshire started to become increasingly aggressive towards the tribes in the south-east including the *Atrebates*[2].

1. Pre-Roman tribes who lived in the Belgium, France and Luxembourg region.
2. Archaeologists have found evidence of small Atrebates settlements on the edge of Chichester city centre.

### Key
— *Future Roman Town Wall*
① *Atrebates settlements*
② *Atrebates roundhouse*

**A** *The Novium Museum*[3]

3. The Novium Museum has a display describing pre-Roman Chichester.

# Contents

2   Introduction/The Romans

4   Chichester 20 CE

6   Chichester 45 CE

8   Chichester 100 CE

10  Chichester 280 CE

12  Chichester 350 CE

14  Chichester 600 CE

16  The Public Bathhouse

18  The Basilica and Forum

20  The Chichester Inscription

22  The Jupiter Stone

24  The Amphitheatre

26  The Roman Theatre

28  The Bosham Head

30  Fishbourne Palace

32  Roman Chichester today

# Symbols used in this guide

**1** Roman site
*(visible remains)*

**2** Roman site
*(no visible remains)*

— Roman wall
*(visible remains)*

— Roman wall
*(no visible remains)*

**3** Speculative Roman site or artefact

— Pre-Roman defences
*(no visible remains)*

**4** Pre-Roman site
*(no visible remains)*

**5** Natural feature

**A** The Novium Museum

**B** Fishbourne Roman Palace and Gardens

*A speculative view of Chichester, looking north, 280 CE.*

## Introduction

Chichester has a long and complex history, spanning nearly two thousand years. Today it is a thriving city dominated by Chichester Cathedral. This guide explores how Chichester evolved from 20 CE to the 6th century CE. In this time it replaced a centre for the local *Atrebates* tribe to become a prosperous Roman town. After this date the Roman Empire started a gradual decline and by 410 CE Britain was under constant attack by marauding Anglo-Saxons. Hundreds of years later Chichester would become part of *Alfred the Great's* network of defended towns which ultimately led to the defeat of the Vikings.

The guide features full-colour 3D illustrations all looking north, while detailed maps help you compare the past with the present.

*Towns and cities*
*The Romans defined towns and cities differently to how we do in the present day. They had three main types of town:*
- *A Colonia, which was a rough equivalent of a city.*
- *A Municipium, which was slightly less important than a colonia.*
- *A Civitas capital, such as Chichester, which was the broad equivalent of a large market town.*

*The Romans called pre-Roman towns 'oppida'.*

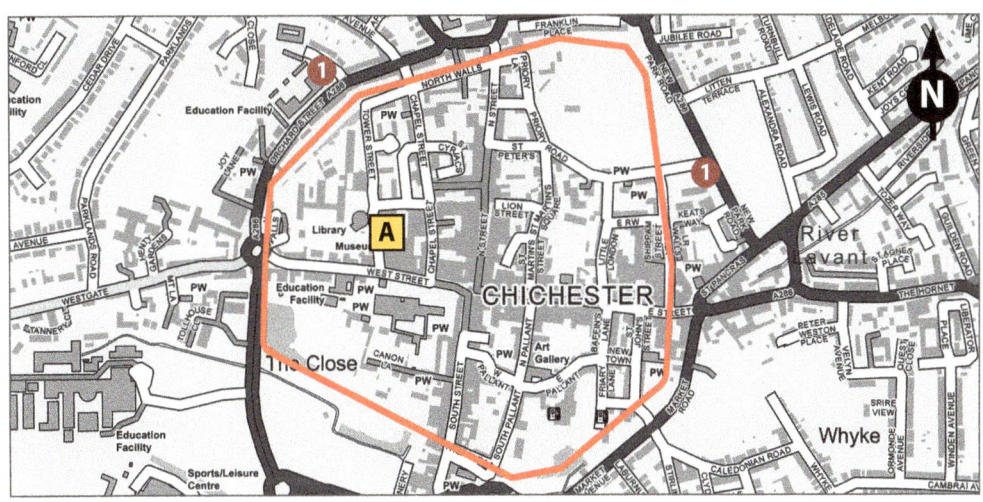

Contains Ordnance Survey data © Crown copyright and database right 2026

*A speculative view of Chichester, looking north, 45 CE.*

# Chichester 45 CE

Four Legions were deployed to invade southern Britain in 43 CE, initially targeting Camulodunum *(Colchester)*. Then approximately 5000 men of the *Legio II Augusta (2nd Legion 'Augustus')* moved south-west from Camulodunum *(Colchester)* into the Chichester area around 44 CE. Chichester was used as a staging area for the invasion of the Isle of Wight about 30 miles *(48 km)* south-west. The Romans needed to take the Isle of Wight before they could move to occupy south-west England. Around 46 CE the main body of the *Legio II Augusta* had moved on, leaving Chichester as a small harbour and storage area for military supplies. Soon after King Togidubnus *(see overleaf)* decided to make the area where Chichester now stands his new centre of power.

## Key

— *Future Roman Town Wall*
❶ *Roman Army legionaries*[1]

[A] *The Novium Museum*[2]

1. The main image shows a speculative view of Roman legionaries marching east.
2. The Novium Museum has displays showing equipment used by the Roman legionaries.

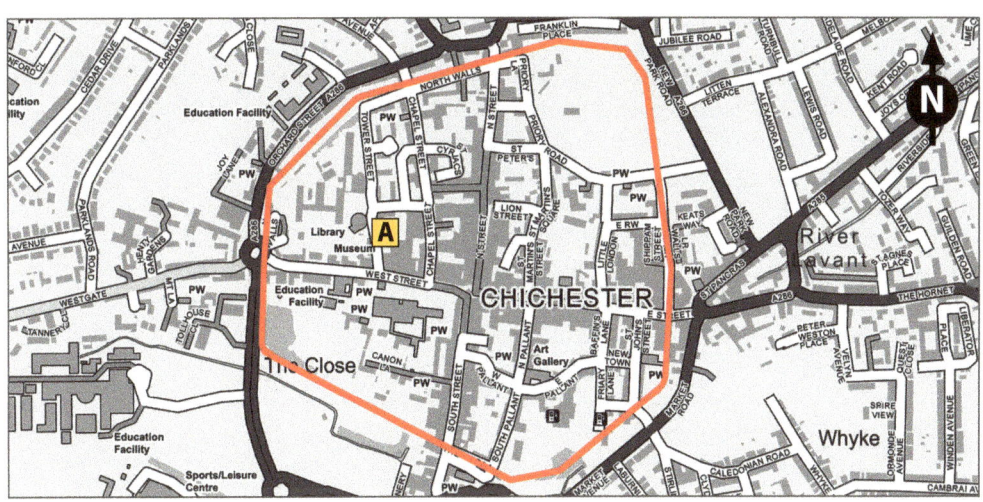

Contains Ordnance Survey data © Crown copyright and database right 2026

*A speculative view of Chichester, looking north, 100 CE.*

# Chichester 100 CE

By this time many public buildings, probably built by King Togidubnus[1], had been constructed, such as an amphitheatre to entertain the locals, along with a public Bathhouse, a temple and a theatre. Most of the houses were probably built from wood and some would have been gradually upgraded as the years passed. From around 50 CE the town was known as Noviomagus Reginorum[2]. Outside of the centre, villas were built for Atrebates nobles, including a significant one at Fishbourne, 3.5 miles (6 km) west.

1. He is thought to have been the equivalent of a king, who was allowed to rule south-east England under the watchful eye of the Romans. The 'palace' at Fishbourne may have been his.
2. Noviomagus Reginorum is thought to mean 'New market of the proud people'.

### Key
— *Future Roman Town Wall*
① *Public Bathhouse*
② *Amphitheatre*
③ *Temple of Neptune and Minerva*
④ *Basilica/Forum*
⑤ *Theatre*

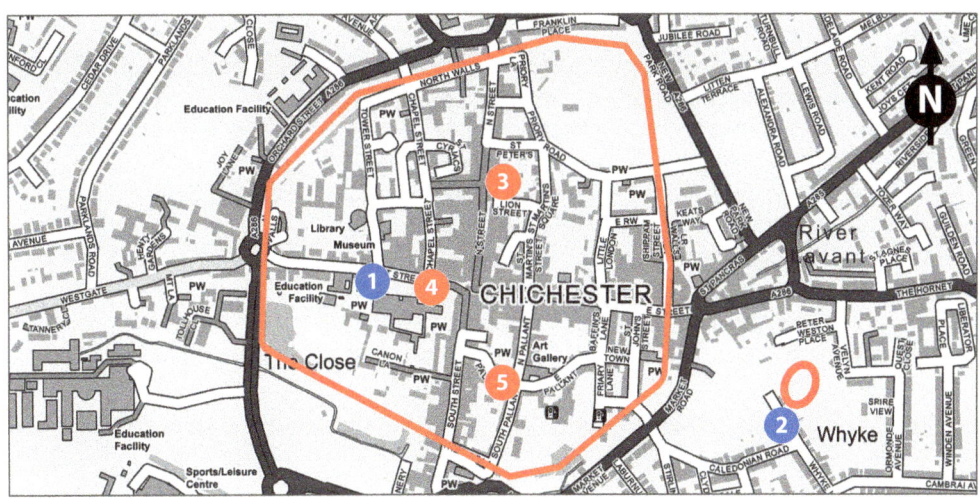

Contains Ordnance Survey data © Crown copyright and database right 2026

# 10. Chichester 280 CE

*A speculative view of Chichester, looking north, 280 CE.*

## Chichester 280 CE

By 280 CE the boundaries of the town had been upgraded, with stone walls, earthen ramparts and a v-shaped ditch. The walls were probably white-washed, with red lines suggesting large blocks. Large sections of Chichester's 7m *(22 feet)* high Roman Town Wall can be seen as shown on the map. The blue lines show what can be seen today, while the red lines show the parts of the wall which are no longer visible. Where the roads met the walls, gatehouses were built to control the passage of people and goods into Roman Chichester. The main image also shows the roads which connected Roman Chichester with London, Fishbourne, Silchester[1], Selsey[2] and Apuldram.[2]

1. A village near Basingstoke.
2. These roads presumably led to Roman harbours close to the modern town of Selsey and the village of Apuldram.

### Key

— Roman Wall
— Visible Roman Wall
1. Southgate
2. Westgate
3. Northgate
4. Eastgate
5. Upgraded defences
6. Cemetery
7. Road to Fishbourne
8. Road to Silchester
9. Road to London
10. Roads to Selsey and Apuldram

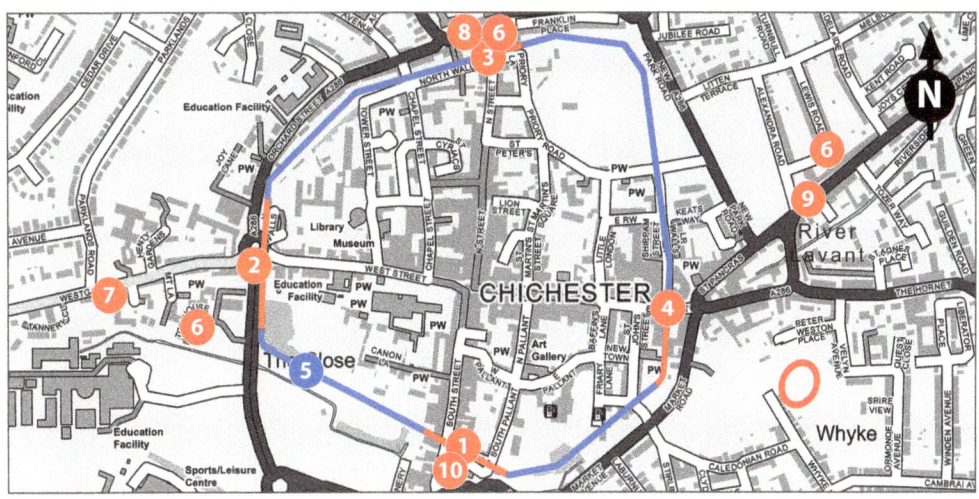

Contains Ordnance Survey data © Crown copyright and database right 2026

# 12. Chichester 350 CE

*A speculative view of Chichester, looking north, 350 CE.*

## Chichester 350 CE

By 350 CE the town wall had been modified in two main ways. The first was the ditch system, which was now much wider and positioned further out from the wall. The second modification was a set of bastions, which may have been up to 12m *(39 feet)* high. Bastions were huge stone towers connected to the wall, which housed heavy weapons called *ballistae*[1] to defend the town. By 367 CE increasing raids by barbarians[2] were taking place along the English Channel and the southern parts of the North Sea, showing the need for improved defences. By 410 CE most of the Romans had left, leaving Britain alone against the barbarian threat.

1. Ballistae were huge crossbows that by the 4th century could fire bolts further than 1,100 metres (1,200 yards).
2. Barbarians included Saxons from northern Europe.

### Key
▬ Roman Wall
▬ Visible Roman Wall
① Bastion[1] *(still visible)*
② Bastion *(no longer visible)*
③ Extended defensive ditch

1. Only a few of the bastions are still visible today, while there may have been as many as seventy. Although evidence of a few bastions has been found, the easiest to see are marked on the map.

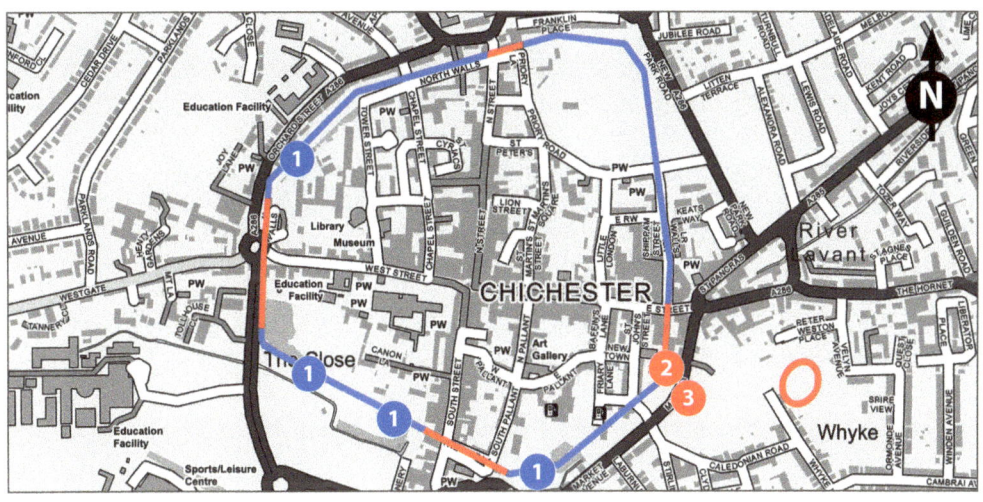

*Contains Ordnance Survey data © Crown copyright and database right 2026*

14. Chichester 600 CE

*A speculative view of Chichester, looking north, 600 CE.*

# Chichester 600 CE

After 410 CE the Roman Army had been withdrawn from Roman Britain as the Roman Empire was under constant attack from internal and external forces. Gradually people moved away from the town and it slowly started to become overgrown ruins. Anglo-Saxon settlers tended to avoid living in the ruins of Roman towns. An 8th or 9th century poem called *The Ruin*[1] captures the Anglo-Saxon's fear and wonder of these once highly advanced towns:
*This masonry is wondrous; · fates broke it, courtyard pavements were smashed; · the work of giants is decaying...'*
The Roman wall which surrounded the town would be reused again, by *Alfred the Great* in his fight against the Vikings in the 9th century.

1. It is thought that 'The Ruin' was written about Roman Bath but could equally apply to other towns such as Chichester.

## Key
■ Roman Wall
■ Visible Roman Wall
① Public Bathhouse ruins
② Bastion ruins
③ Amphitheatre ruins
④ Basilica ruins
⑤ Roman Theatre ruins
⑥ Gatehouse ruins
⑦ Temple ruins

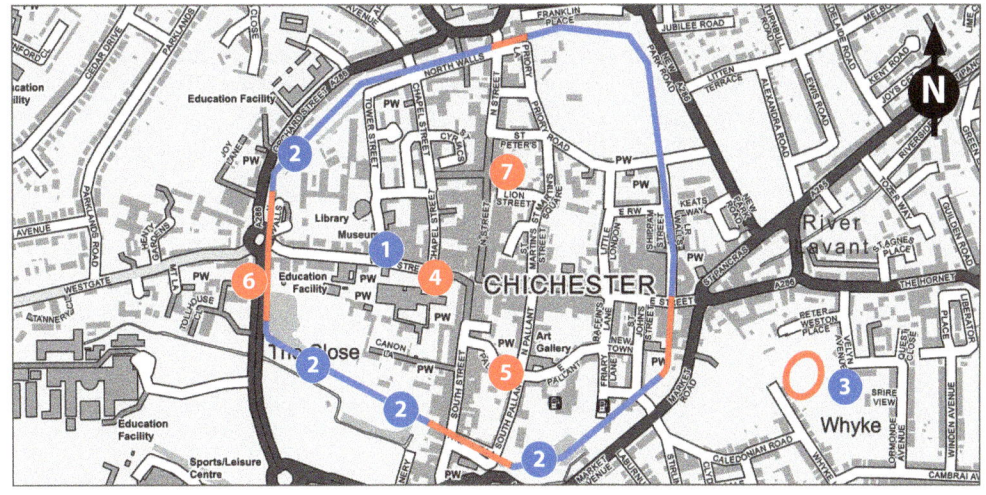

*Contains Ordnance Survey data © Crown copyright and database right 2026*

*A speculative view of the Public Bathhouse, looking north, 280 CE.*

## The Public Bathhouse

*Noviomagus Reginorum* had an impressive bathhouse located in the centre of the town. It would have had a furnace to heat the *Caldarium (hot room)* and the *Tepidarium (warm room)*. There was also a *Frigidarium (cold room)*, and a large *Palaestra (exercise area)*. People typically bathed and socialised, in some ways like in our present day swimming pools. The Romans did not have soap products, so instead used oil and scraped the oil off with a curved implement called a strigil. The bathhouse may have had many other facilities such as an *Apodyterium (heated changing rooms)* and possibly a library.

It may have been built around 70 CE as part of the collection of impressive public buildings constructed by King Togidubnus (see page 8) and was uncovered in 1974/75 as part of construction work in the city centre.

### Key

- ▬ Roman Wall
- ▬ Visible Roman Wall
- ❶ Public Bathhouse
- ❷ Caldarium
- ❸ Tepidarium
- ❹ Frigidarium
- ❺ Palaestra
- ❻ Apodyterium
- ❼ Cistern (water tank)
- 🄰 The Novium Museum[1]

1. A large section of the of the Public Bathhouse is on display inside the museum.

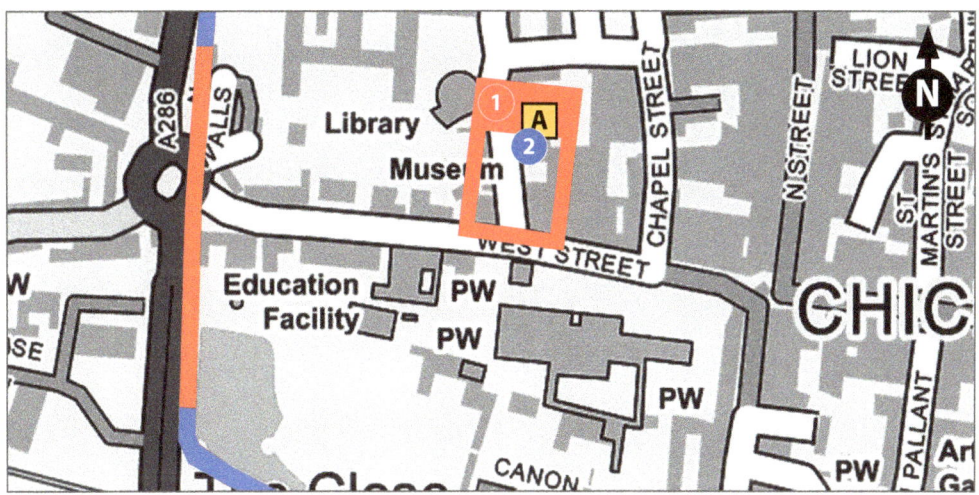

*Contains Ordnance Survey data © Crown copyright and database right 2026*

*A speculative view of the Basilica and Forum, looking north, 280 CE.*

## The Basilica and Forum

The *Basilica* and *Forum (public square)* were the most important civic structures in major Roman towns. The *Basilica* was the commercial and administrative heart of Roman Chichester, and was where deals were made and laws practised; it was also the regional government office. The exact layout of the site is not known, so a **possible** arrangement is shown on the main image and map. A large statue dedicated to Jupiter may have stood in the Forum *(see page 22)*. There would also have been market stalls selling food and household items sourced from all over the Roman Empire. Some of the merchants who traded here became very rich and built large villas in the surrounding countryside, such as Bignor Villa[1].

1. *Bignor Villa lies 14 miles (23 km) north-east of Chichester and features many fine mosaics.*

### Key

- Roman Wall
- Visible Roman Wall
- ❶ Basilica
- ❷ Forum
- ❸ Statue dedicated to Jupiter
- ❹ Mosaic[2]
- ❺ Temple dedicated to Neptune and Minerva *(see page 20)*

2. *Parts of a mosaic from a building located near to the Basilica/Forum can be seen inside Chichester Cathedral.*

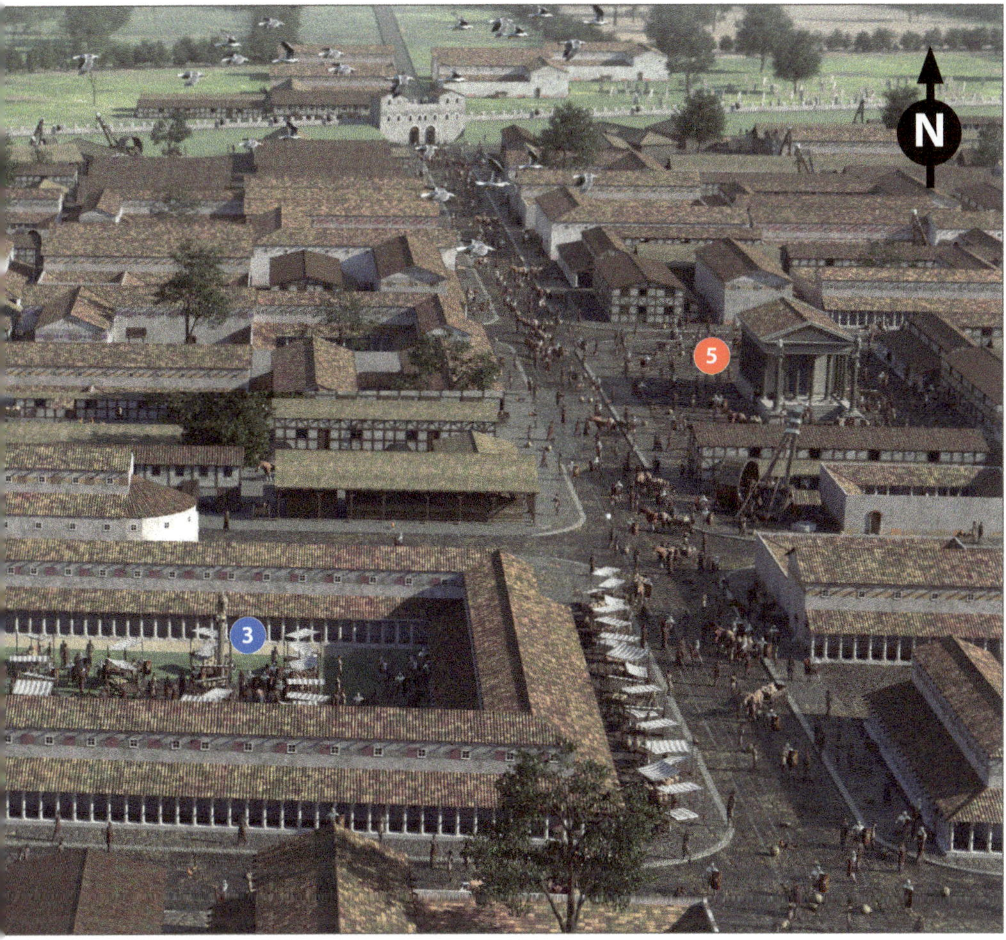

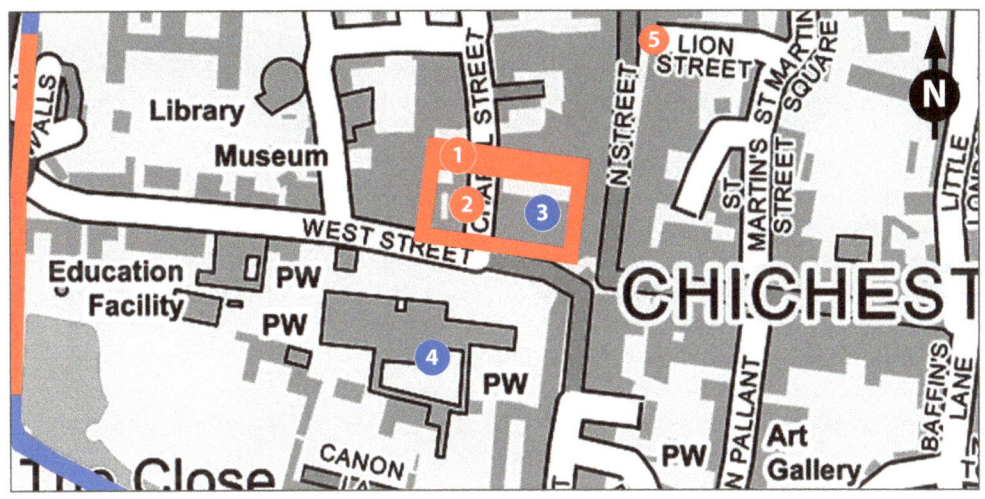

Contains Ordnance Survey data © Crown copyright and database right 2026

*A speculative view of the Chichester inscription in Roman times (left) and how it looks now (right).*

# The Chichester Inscription

In 1723 an inscription dating from around 70 CE was found close to the present day location of the Council Chamber, in North Street. It is one of the most famous inscriptions found in Roman Britain, translated as:

'To Neptune[1] and Minerva[2], for the welfare of the Divine House, by the authority of Tiberius Claudius Togidubnus[3], great king of the Britons, the guild of smiths and those in it gave this temple at their own expense ...ens, son of Pudentinus, presented the site.'

The Purbeck marble inscription, which measures about 1.2m *(3ft)* x 0.8 m *(2.6ft)*, may have been located on the front of a temple dedicated to Neptune and Minerva.

1. Neptune was the Roman god of water and the sea.
2. Minerva was the Roman goddess of wisdom and justice.

## Key
▬ *Roman Wall*
▬ *Visible Roman Wall*
① *The Chichester Inscription[3]*

3. *The position of the Temple of Neptune and Minerva (which the Chichester Inscription was part of) is suggested on the map. An illustration showing how the temple **might** have looked can be seen on page 18.*

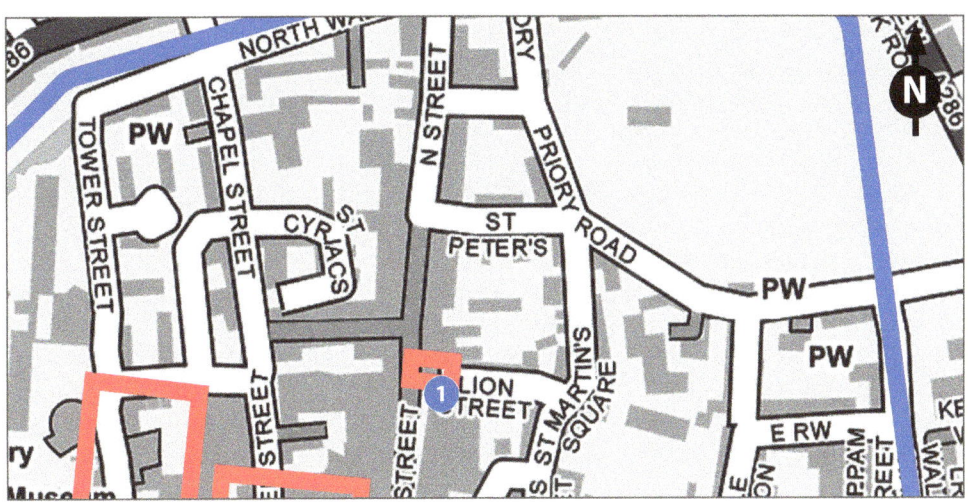

Contains Ordnance Survey data © Crown copyright and database right 2026

*A speculative view of the Jupiter Stone, in Roman times (left) and now (far right).*

# The Jupiter Stone

In 1934 excavations on West Street unearthed a large stone, thought to have been the base of a column topped with a statue dedicated to the god *Jupiter*[1]. This may have stood in front of the town's Basilica *(see page 18), possibly* dating from around 200 CE. On the sides are inscriptions and carvings, the inscription reads:

I O M (IVPITER OPTIMUS MAXIMUS)
IN HONOREM DO MVS DIVINA, which can be translated as:
'To Jupiter Best and Greatest, In Honour of the Divine House'.
The main illustration shows a speculative view of how the statue may have looked and the section of the statue's base[2] that can be seen in the Novium Museum.

1. Jupiter was the Roman king of the gods as well as the god of sky and thunder.
2. Now known as the Jupiter Stone

## Key

- 🟥 Roman Wall
- 🟦 Visible Roman Wall
- ① Jupiter Stone
- ② Statue dedicated to Jupiter[3]
- ③ Basilica (See page 18)
- ④ Forum (See page 18)

- [A] The Novium Museum

3. Note that the location and design of the statue is speculative.

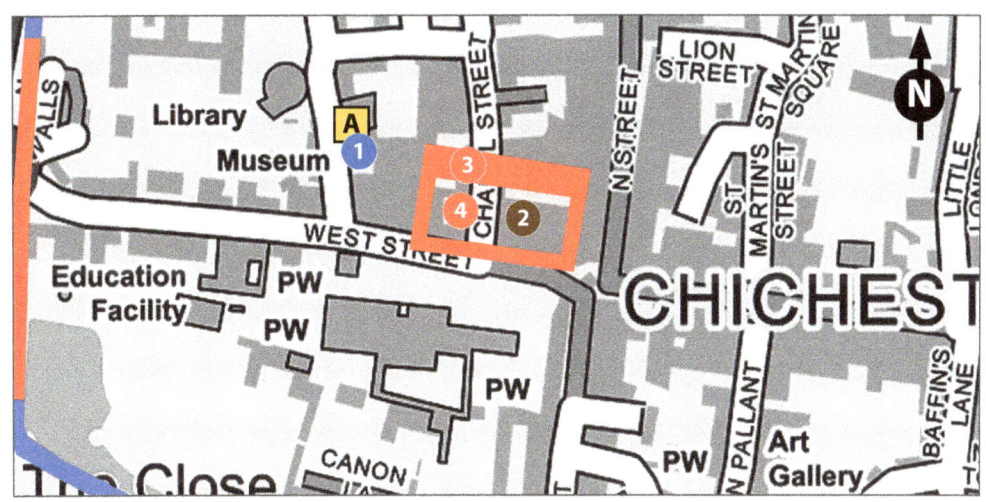

*A speculative view of the Amphitheatre, looking north, 280 CE.*

# The Amphitheatre

Around 70 CE an amphitheatre was built to provide entertainment for the inhabitants of Roman Chichester. Market stalls would have been clustered around the base of the amphitheatre, selling food to the crowds.

Contests usually began with the gladiators *(Latin for swordsmen)* paraded in front of the crowd, with music playing. These contests often started in the morning, with the victors celebrated in the middle of the day.

Bears, wolves, criminals and Christians were all forced to fight in the *'games'* held inside the amphitheatre.

There are minimal remains of the outline of the amphitheatre, located in a small park to the east of the city centre. In addition a small information panel in the park shows how the amphitheatre may have looked. Its position is also marked on the map, see right.

**Key**
- ▬ Roman Wall
- ▬ Visible Roman Wall
- ① Roman Amphitheatre
- ② Vomitorium (entrance/exit)
- ③ Velaria (awnings)
- ④ Cavea (seating)
- ⑤ Arena
- ⑥ Gladiator
- ⑦ Market stalls
- ⑧ Eastgate
- ⑨ Cemetery

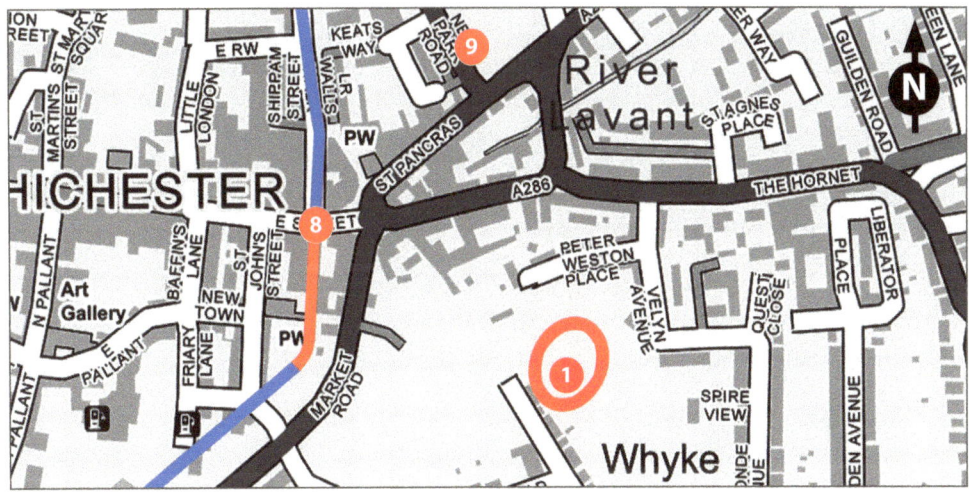

Contains Ordnance Survey data © Crown copyright and database right 2026

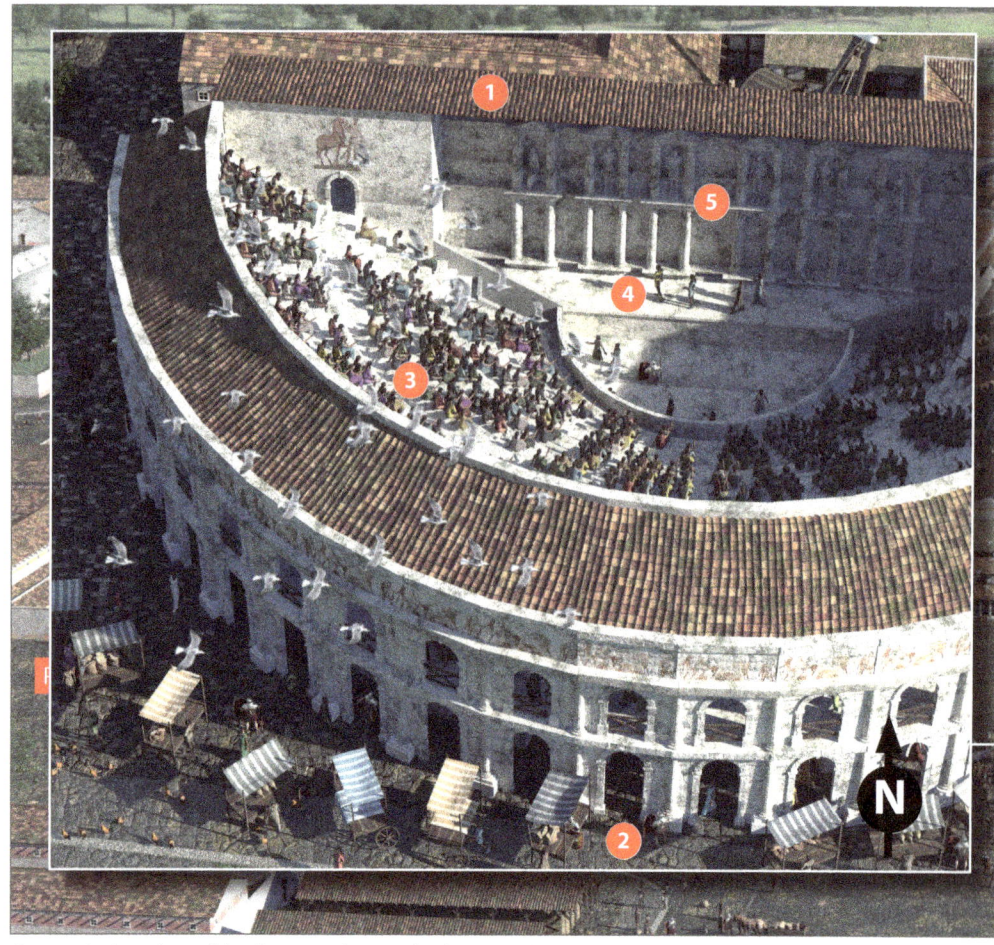

*A speculative view of the Roman Theatre, looking north, 280 CE.*

# The Roman Theatre

Archaeologists believe that a Roman theatre stood in the south of the city centre. Pantomimes were more popular than plays, as well as comedies based on people's lives. The audience would have entered the theatre through the *Vomitorium*[1] and sat in the semi-circular *Auditorium*, overlooking the *Orchestra*[2]. The building may have stood over 20 metres *(60 feet)* tall with a large and complex stage area including the *Scaenae frons*, which was full of columns and provided a background for the actors. Often the actors wore strange masks which represented their characters. Unlike present day actors, Roman actors were not well respected and were often slaves.

1. A passage where crowds could enter and exit the theatre.
2. The theatre stage[2].

**Key**
- Roman Wall
- Visible Roman Wall
- ① Roman Theatre[3]
- ② Vomitorium
- ③ Auditorium
- ④ Orchestra
- ⑤ Scaenae frons

3. It is not known exactly what the Roman theatre in Chichester looked like, the main image shows a speculative view based on the Roman theatre found in the centre of Colchester.

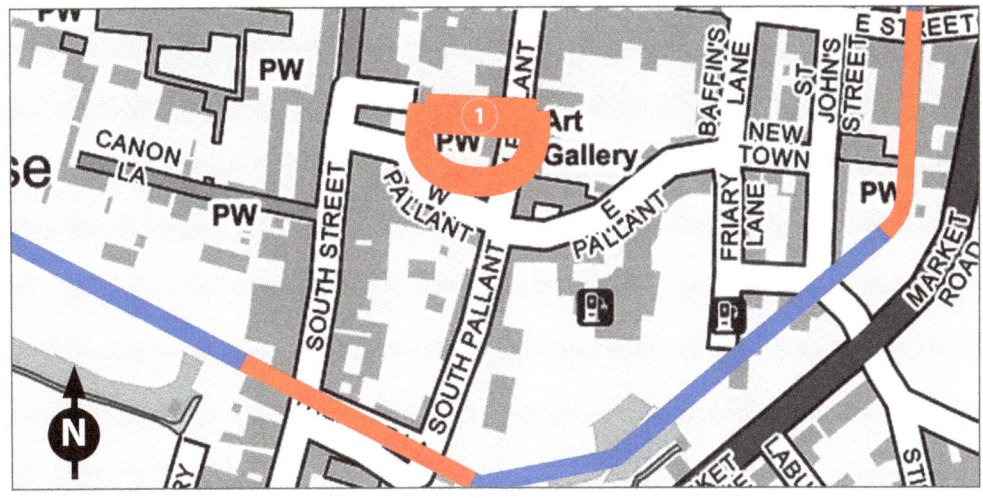

Contains Ordnance Survey data © Crown copyright and database right 2026

*A speculative view of the Bosham Head in 200 CE, and how it **might** have degraded.*

# The Bosham Head

The Bosham Head was discovered[1] in a vicarage garden in the coastal village of Bosham 6 miles *(10 km)* west of Chichester. It is thought that it **might** have been part of a twice life-sized statue of the Emperor *Trajan*, although as it is so damaged there is debate that it may have depicted a different emperor. The statue might have been situated at the entrance to Chichester harbour. As the centuries passed, the marble head fell from the body and was eroded by storms and sunshine, until now it has become very difficult to see any distinct features. Detailed 3D scans performed recently led to the view that it may date from approximately the late 1st century or early 2nd century.

1. It is not known exactly when the head was discovered, but an engraving from 1824 shows the head inside a vicarage garden.

### Key

1. The Bosham Head, now[2]
2. Speculative statue of the Emperor Trajan
3. Speculative column
4. Person to scale

**A** The Novium Museum

1. The Bosham Head is on display at the Novium Museum.

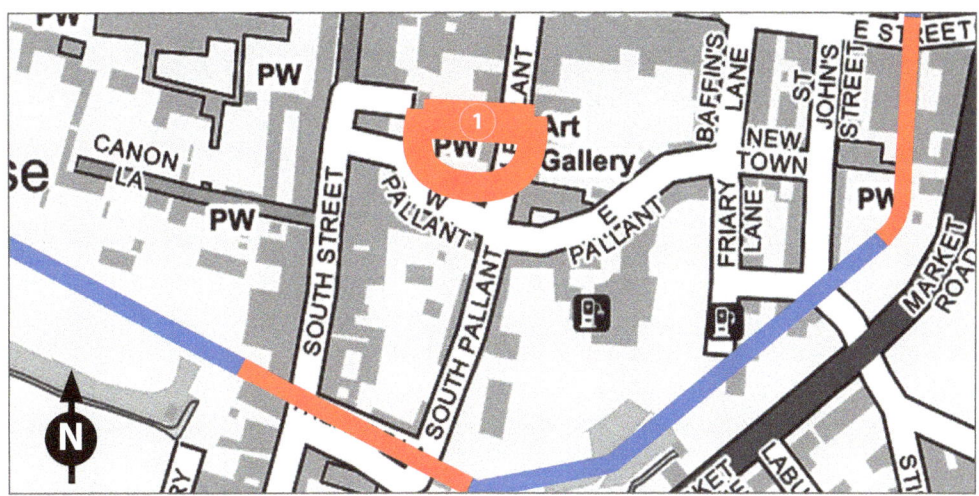

Contains Ordnance Survey data © Crown copyright and database right 2026

*A speculative view of the Bosham Head in 200 CE, and how it **might** have degraded.*

# The Bosham Head

The Bosham Head was discovered[1] in a vicarage garden in the coastal village of Bosham 6 miles *(10 km)* west of Chichester. It is thought that it **might** have been part of a twice life-sized statue of the Emperor *Trajan*, although as it is so damaged there is debate that it may have depicted a different emperor. The statue might have been situated at the entrance to Chichester harbour. As the centuries passed, the marble head fell from the body and was eroded by storms and sunshine, until now it has become very difficult to see any distinct features. Detailed 3D scans performed recently led to the view that it may date from approximately the late 1st century or early 2nd century.

1. It is not known exactly when the head was discovered, but an engraving from 1824 shows the head inside a vicarage garden.

### Key
1. The Bosham Head, now[2]
2. Speculative statue of the Emperor Trajan
3. Speculative column
4. Person to scale

**A** The Novium Museum

1. The Bosham Head is on display at the Novium Museum.

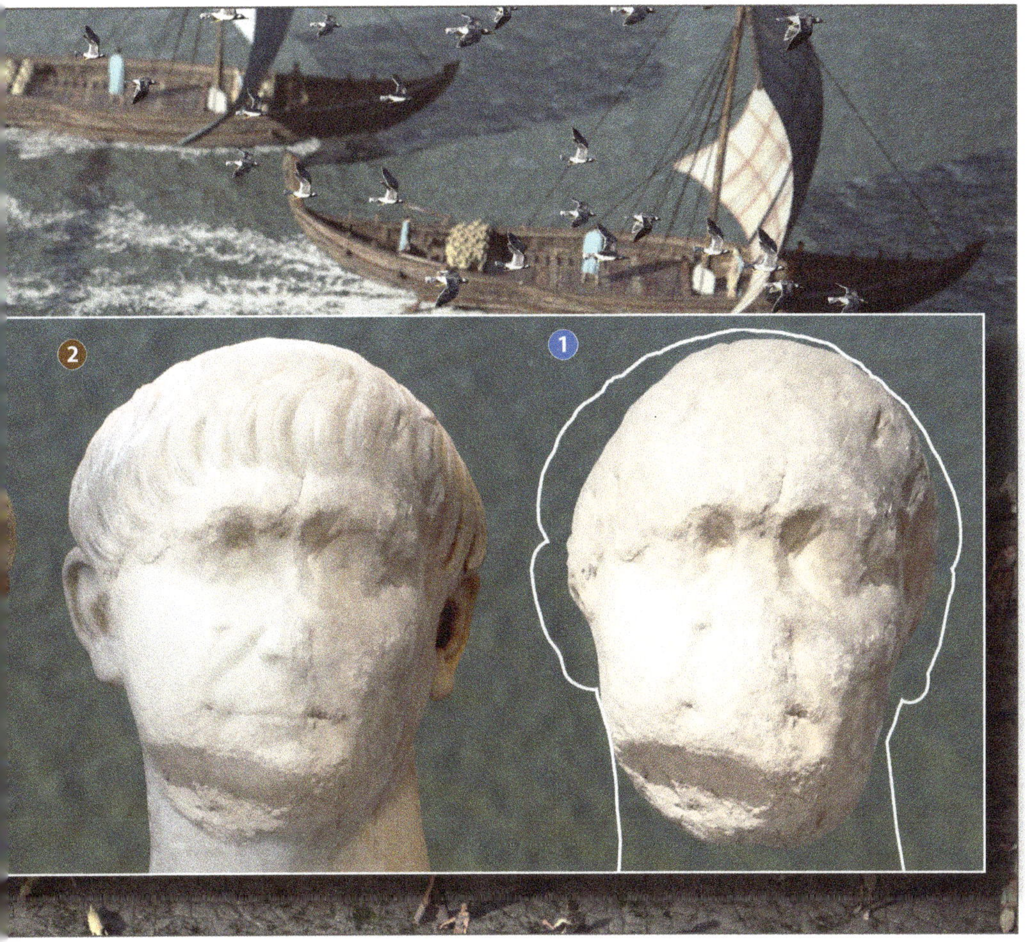

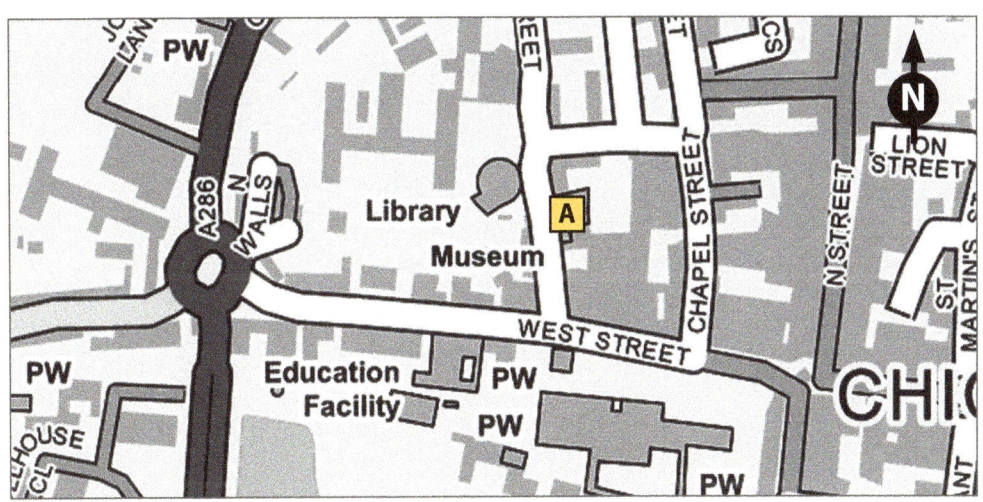

*A speculative view of Fishbourne Palace and Roman Chichester, looking north, around 100 CE.*

# Fishbourne Palace

About 3 miles *(5 km)* to the west of Chichester lies the remains of a significant Roman palace. It was discovered by accident by workmen digging a water trench. Over time, as the site was unearthed by archaeologists, some of the finest Roman mosaics in Britain were uncovered. The site is thought to have started just after the Roman invasion of 43 CE as a small military supply base before a large 'palace' was constructed. It is thought to have been built by King Togidubnus[1] around 75-80 CE. The palace would have had large gardens and probably many people to run and maintain it. Some of the palace was destroyed around 270 CE. The main image also shows the site of another Roman villa nearby and Roman Chichester to the east.

1. See page 8 and page 20 for further details.

### Key

- Extent of Roman Chichester and Fishbourne Palace
- ① Fishbourne Palace
- ② Roman Villa
- ③ River
- ④ Chichester harbour (in Roman times)
- ⑤ Roman ship
- B Fishbourne Roman Palace and Gardens museum which has many fine mosaics, displays and artefacts.

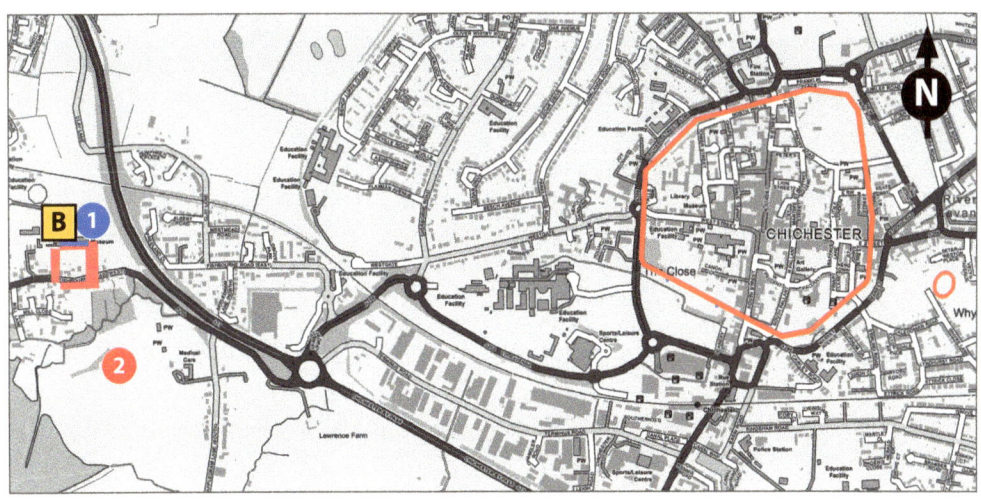

*Contains Ordnance Survey data © Crown copyright and database right 2026*

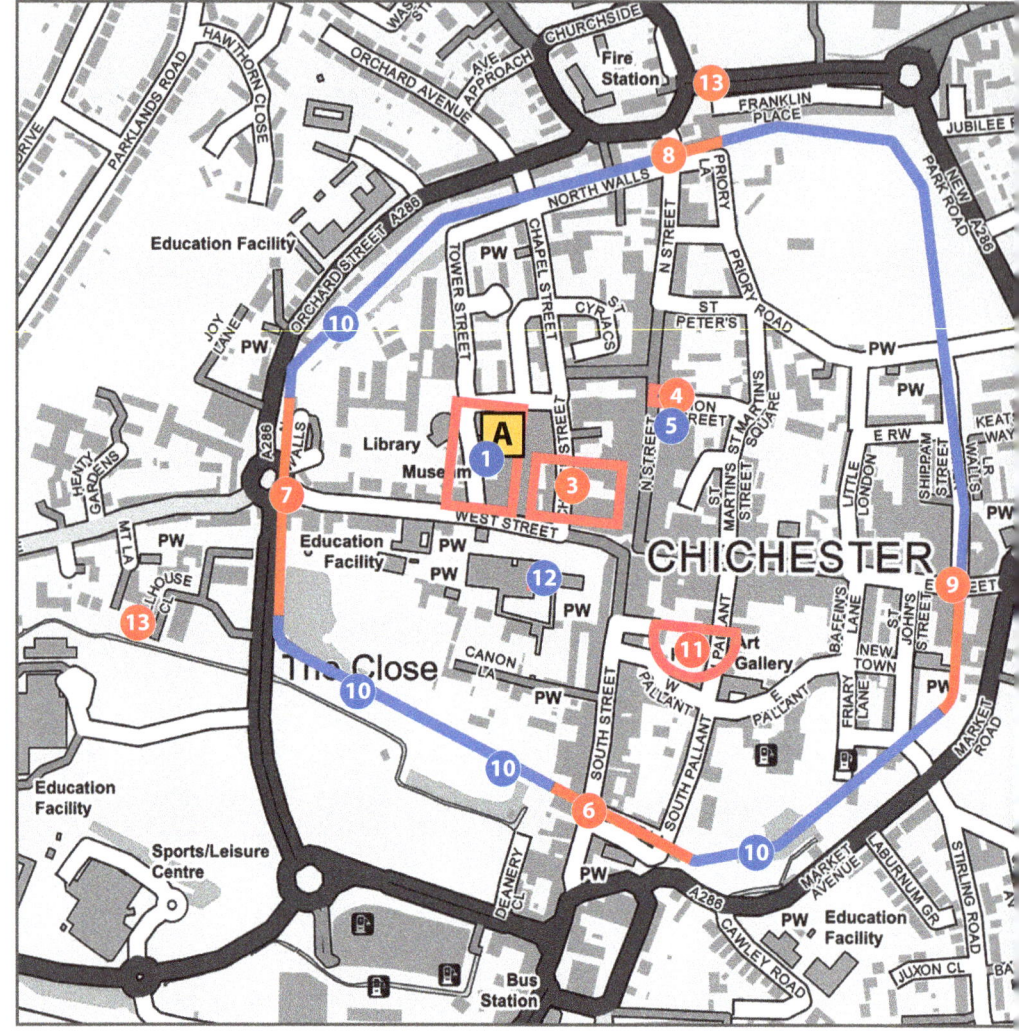

# Roman Chichester today

Most of *Roman Chichester* is now no longer visible, except for large sections of the Roman Wall. The Novium Museum *(yellow square)* has a large section of the Public Bathhouse, artefacts and displays.

There are minimal remains of the Roman Amphitheatre and an information board.

All the exterior images in this book face north, so that you can compare the past with the present day maps.

*About 3 miles (5 km) to the west of Chichester is the Fishbourne Roman Palace and Gardens museum, which has many fine Roman mosaics, and much more.*

**Key**
- **1** Roman site *(visible remains)*
- **2** Roman site *(no visible remains)*
- — Roman wall *(visible remains)*
- — Roman wall *(no visible remains)*

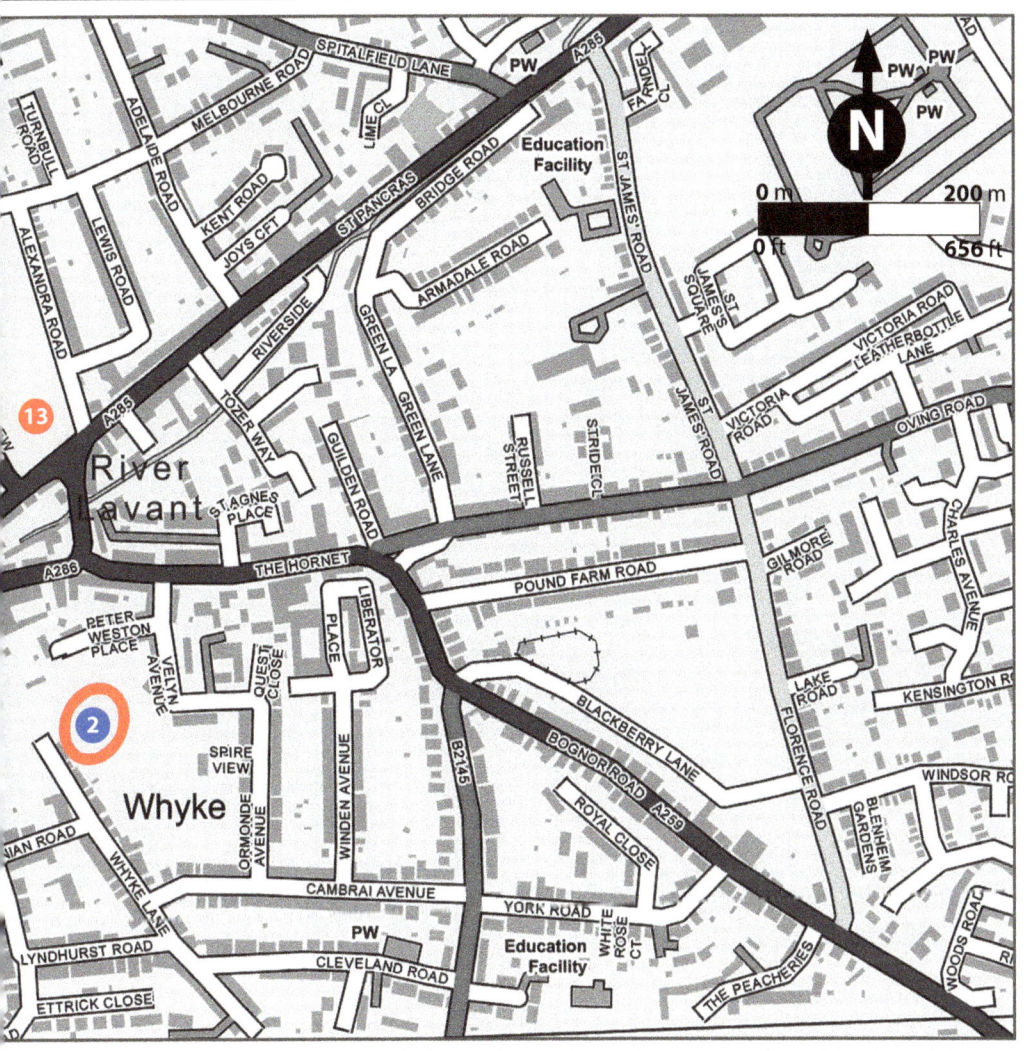

Contains Ordnance Survey data © Crown copyright and database right 2026

- Town Wall
  *(page 10/12)*
- Town Wall
  *(page 10/12)*
- ① Public Bathhouse
  *(page 16)*
- ② Amphitheatre
  *(page 24)*
- ③ Basilica/Forum
  *(page 18)*
- ④ Roman Temple
  *(page 18)*
- ⑤ Chichester Inscription
  *(page 20)*
- ⑥ Southgate
  *(page 10)*
- ⑦ Westgate
  *(page 10)*
- ⑧ Northgate
  *(page 10)*
- ⑨ Eastgate
  *(page 10)*
- ⑩ Roman Bastion
  *(page 12)*
- ⑪ Roman Theatre
  *(page 26)*
- ⑫ Roman mosaic
  *(page 18)*
- ⑬ Roman cemetery
  *(page 10)*

- A The Novium Museum
  The Jupiter Stone
  *(pages 18/22)*
  The Bosham Head
  *(page 28)*

First published January 2024
ISBN 978-1-7391254-7-9 *(Paperback)*
Second Edition, published January 2026

Designed and published by JC3DVIS
www.jc3dvis.co.uk
Book design © 2026 Joseph Chittenden

All the images in this guide were produced by JC3DVIS.
Contains Ordnance Survey data © Crown copyright and database right 2026
The moral right of the copyright holder has been asserted.

All rights reserved. No part of this publication may be reproduced, distributed or transmitted in any form or by any means, including photocopying, recording, or other electronic or mechanical methods, without the prior written permission of the publisher.

**With special thanks to:**
James Kenny, *Archaeology Officer, Chichester District Council*
Mark Elliot, *Travel Writer*
Jane Chittenden

**Legal disclaimer**
Neither the author nor the publisher shall be held liable or responsible to any person or entity with respect to any loss or incidental or consequential damages caused, or alleged to have been caused, directly or indirectly, by the information contained herein.

**Principal source consulted**
• James Kenny Archaeology Officer, Chichester District Council

**Bibliography and other sources**
• Chichester Cathedral website: *The Roman Mosaics*
• City Walls Partnership: *Chichester City Walls, A legacy of the Romans*
• Cunliffe, Barry: *Fishbourne Roman Palace*
• Dawkes, Giles and Hart, Diccon: *Chichester Thermae reconsidered (accessed online)*
• Historic England website: *Monument number 924355 (Temple of Neptune)*
• Historic England website: *Roman amphitheatre, Chichester-1002984*
• https://romaninscriptionsofbritain.org/inscriptions/91 *(Chichester inscription)*
• Manley, Harry & Russell, Miles:-*Trajan Places: Establishing identity and context for the Bosham and Hawkshaw heads (accessed online)*
• Margary, Ivan D: *Roman Roads in Britain, Volume one*
• Rudkin, David: *Fishbourne Roman Palace*
• *Visit to Fishbourne Roman Palace and Gardens museum*
• *Visit to The Novium Museum*

www.ingramcontent.com/pod-product-compliance
Lightning Source LLC
Chambersburg PA
CBHW042321090526
44585CB00024BA/2781